This book is dedicated to Corinne, Timothy, Olivia and all the children that love someone with a sickness that you can't see. You guys are my heroes.

My name is Corinne and I'm the oldest Sister. I love to dance and hang out with my friends. My little brother and sister drive me crazy, but I love them so much.

This is my sister Olivia.
She loves to play dress up in mom's dresses and high heels while singing, and she never stops talking.

This my brother Timothy. He is quiet and loves to play football. He is also really good at jujitsu.

And this is our story...

We love to go to our Grammy and Grampy's house.
Mom takes us whenever we want and we love to sleep over.
They have all kinds of snacks for us; like Grammy's
homemade brownies, and Grampy's famous ice cream
sundaes.

We stay up late and watch funny movies together. Sometimes we create videos of us singing and dancing to silly songs. Sometimes we play hide and seek outside.

Grammy and Grampy are the best. They always take us to our favorite spot in New Hampshire for the weekend. We play in the pool and we go for rides on the tall mountains. We look for moose, deer and bear. Olivia never stops talking for the whole ride. Olivia's chattering drives Timothy and me crazy! Grammy tells us we deserve to go on vacation.

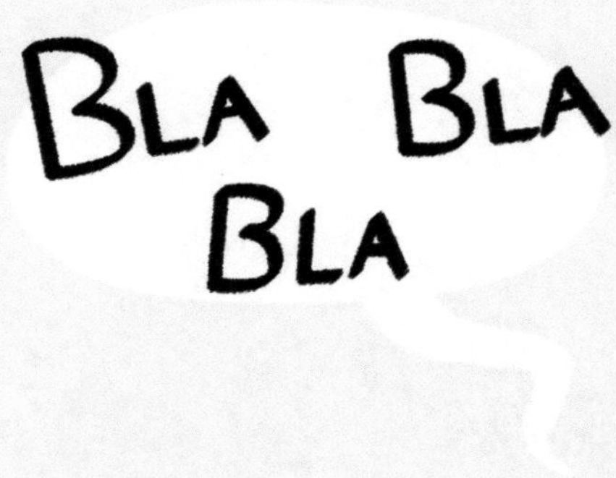
BLA BLA BLA

Our Dad's name is Patrick. We love him so much. He is silly and always does funny things like telling us funny jokes and stories. Sometimes, he lives at our Grammy and Grampy's house. We are so happy when he is there because then we get to see him.

HA HA HA HA HA H

When I was two years old, all I wanted to do was play with
the toilet plunger. Dad bought me my very own plunger to
play with. He used to laugh all the time. He would make
everyone else laugh too. He has the biggest laugh and the
best smile.

Olivia always sat with Dad. She quietly followed him everywhere. He always watched movies with us about dragons, wizards and magic.

He always made us his famous macaroni and cheese. It is so good. We would love to go to Grammy and Grampy's house just to be with him.

There is something different about Dad though. My dad is sick, but, you can't see his sickness. If you looked at my Dad you would think he was healthy, but he is not.

My Grammy is a nurse and she knows all about sick people. She tells us that somebody can be sick, but not look sick. When he is sick he walks around the house like he has ants in his pants, he doesn't tell his funny jokes, he gets angry easy, and then... he leaves.

We know Dad is really sick when he is not living at Grammy and Grampy's. Mom tells us the sickness is called addiction and its invisible.

Sometimes Dad is gone for a while and my brother, sister and me don't see him. This makes us sad. One time we did not see Dad for a whole year. It made us cry.

When we don't see Dad for awhile, we know he is sick again. We really miss him so much.

We miss him so much.
To make us feel better, we do the things that he loves to do
with us so it makes us happy again. We watch his favorite
movies or tell his funny jokes to each other.
But it is not the same.

Dad loves to climb mountains and lift weights. When he is healthy he climbs the highest mountains and lifts the heaviest weights. When my dad is sick he doesn't do any of that. He just wants to sleep and he doesn't look very strong.

We still love him very much.

Sometimes when Dad is sick we can hear Mom and Grammy talking about how mad they are at him and that makes us sad. We are not mad at him.
We just really miss him.

My Mom says that Dad may get better one day, and maybe he won't.

It's not our fault that he is sick. We are not embarrassed about our Dad's sickness because everyone loves someone that has been sick before. Dad loves us so much no matter how sick he gets. Loving someone that has a sickness you can't see is not always easy.

WE LOVE YOU DADDY

Made in United States
Troutdale, OR
10/25/2024

23948254R00017